Written by Tori Kosara

Designed by Angie Allison
Edited by Hannah Cohen, Jen Wainwright and Philippa Wingate
Production by Joanne Rooke
Picture Research by Judith Palmer

With thanks to Morgan-Lilly Duffield

Picture Acknowledgements

Front cover: Getty Images
Back cover: Sara Jaye/ Rex Features

Getty Images: pages 8, 9, 15, 26, 38/39, 41
FilmMagic/Getty Images: pages 2/3, 25, 50/51, 62/63
Michael Ochs Archives/Getty Images: page 46
Redferns/Getty Images: pages 16/17
WireImage/Getty Images: pages 6, 11, 12, 29, 34, 36, 47, 54, 57
Francis Specker/LANDOV/Press Association Images: pages 32, 42
Sara Jaye/Rex Features: pages 31, 53

Published in Great Britain in 2010 by Buster Books,
an imprint of Michael O'Mara Books Limited,
9 Lion Yard, Tremadoc Road, London SW4 7NQ

www.mombooks.com/busterbooks

A CIP catalogue record for this book is available from the British Library.

ISBN: 978-1-907151-40-8

1 3 5 7 9 10 8 6 4 2

This book was printed in July 2010 at L.E.G.O., Viale dell'Industria 2, 36100, Vicenza, Italy.

JUSTIN BIEBER
ANNUAL 2011
>>> >>> UNAUTHORIZED >>

Buster Books

CONTENTS

INTRODUCING JUSTIN BIEBER

People across the world have caught Bieber Fever! With a truly devoted fan-base, Justin Bieber has gone from a pre-teen YouTube celebrity to a 16-year-old international pop star in no time at all.

BIGGER AND BETTER

During his incredibly fast rise to fame, Justin has appeared on TV and radio shows all around the world. He has even starred in his own TV show – *The Diary of Justin Bieber* – on MTV in the USA.

Justin has made it into the top ten list of the USA's most-downloaded songs on iTunes and millions of copies of his singles and albums have been snatched up by adoring fans.

The star's tunes have rocketed to the top of the music charts, making him the youngest US chart-topper in nearly 50 years.

ALL ACCESS PASS

This book gives you the chance to get up-close-and-personal with Justin.

Find out about his love life, his songs and his most embarrassing secrets. Read how Justin made it from the internet to the international stage, peek into his personal style-file and much, much more!

This is just the start. The road ahead holds many golden opportunities for Justin, who is travelling straight to the top.

JUST THE FACTS

NAME: Justin Drew Bieber

DATE OF BIRTH: 1st March 1994

EYES: Brown

STAR SIGN: Pisces

FAMILY FEATURES: He has his dad's eyes and nose and his mum's lips

FAVE COLOUR: Purple

NATIONALITY: Canadian

HOME TOWN: Stratford, Ontario, Canada

LIVES: Atlanta, Georgia, USA

SIBLINGS: A younger half-sister, named Jazmyn, and a younger half-brother, named Jaxon

RECORD LABEL: Island Records

PETS: A papillon pooch named Sammy

INSTRUMENTS: Trumpet, guitar, piano and drums

STYLE: Skater cool

MUSICAL INFLUENCES: Usher, Michael Jackson, Stevie Wonder, Boyz II Men

HOBBIES: Playing sports, skateboarding and breakdancing

LANGUAGES SPOKEN: English and French

FAVE FOODS: Spaghetti bolognaise, cheesecake and 'Sour Patch Kids' sweets

EATS FOR BREAKFAST: Cap'n Crunch cereal

FEARS: Confined spaces and large crowds

LOVES: Going to the movies with friends and playing Nintendo

HATES: Ugg boots on girls

FAVE MOVIE: *Rocky IV*

FAVE TV SHOW: *Smallville*

AMBITIONS: To perform a duet with Beyoncé, go to college, and break into acting

FAVE SUPERHERO: Superman

RIGHT- OR LEFT-HANDED? Left-handed

MAC OR PC? Mac

JUSTIN ON ...

... LOVE

"I think it feels good. I mean, I'm not an expert about love or anything. I'm still learning, I'm still trying to get the process."

... SCHOOL

"I'm doing a lot of schoolwork online, and my tutor sometimes travels with me, so I still get my schoolwork done."

... HIS RISE TO FAME

"My head was definitely spinning. I was like, 'Am I dreaming?' It was kind of a surreal moment."

... HIS DREAM JOB

"I'd like to be an architect. That would be cool. I like drawing."

... WHO HE'D LIKE TO HAVE LUNCH WITH

"Chuck Norris."

... HIS FAVOURITE WEBSITE

"Freetypinggame.net. I don't know why I'm obsessed with it."

... DREAMING

"I don't dream. I just fall asleep, see black, and wake up."

BIEBER BEGINS

From belting out tunes in the comfort of his own home, to his first meeting with record label executives – here's how Justin got started in the music biz.

THE STORY STARTS

When he was 12 years old, Justin entered a talent competition in his home town in Ontario, Canada. Most of the other contestants were trained by vocal coaches, but Justin, who hadn't had lessons, managed to win second place. "I wasn't taking it too seriously at the time," he admitted. "I would just sing around the house."

VIDEO SENSATION

Justin's new-found success made him keen to share his songs with other people. He loved singing songs by recording artists such as Stevie Wonder, Ne-Yo and Usher (shown here). So, in 2007, he decided to film himself singing his own sensational versions of these music superstars' hits. He posted the videos online for his friends and family to enjoy.

Then something unexpected happened – people Justin didn't know began tuning into his videos and loving them. Justin's video performances racked up ten million hits in just seven months.

CHANCE MEETING

Scooter Braun, a managing executive from So So Def Recordings, heard about the talented vocalist who was getting so much attention online. He flew Justin to his offices in Atlanta. By chance they bumped into Usher in a car park and persuaded him to come and listen to Justin perform. But Usher failed to show up. "I always tease Usher now and remind him how he blew me off the first time we met," Justin says.

It wasn't long, however, before Usher invited Justin back to Atlanta, and asked him to sign a record deal.

Justin was signed to Island Records in 2008. Scooter became his manager and Usher handed Justin the opportunity of a lifetime – a great start in the music business.

BIEBER FEVER!

NEWSFLASH! Close to 40 million fans are suffering from 'Bieber Fever'. The symptoms are a racing pulse, uncontrollable giggles and a big, big smile whenever Justin's around. Female fans around the world have named themselves 'Biebettes', and they've done some crazy things to catch his eye.

TEARS FOR JUSTIN

A three-year-old girl named Cody faced a home-video camera with tears streaming down her face. When asked why she was crying, she said, "Because I love Justin Bieber."

Justin saw the video on YouTube, and later surprised the tearful tot on a TV talk show called *Jimmy Kimmel Live!* Lucky Cody met Justin and hugged him with a huge smile on her face. She even asked him to marry her!

CAMPING OUT

When Justin appeared on a morning TV show called *The Today Show*, some fans camped outside the studio for up to 32 hours before the performance. The wait was worth it for these dedicated fans, because Justin made time to meet as many of them as he could before going on stage.

When Justin travelled to the UK for his first promotional tour, he was mobbed by British fans. He signed autographs and greeted lots of people – some of whom had been waiting for hours for him to arrive.

RISKY BUSINESS

The Bieber Fever epidemic has spread to Australia, too. Justin was due to play at an outdoor concert for a morning TV show in Sydney. Four thousand fans camped out overnight to catch Justin's performance. When he appeared, ten fans got crushed as people rushed forward to get as close to the stage as possible. The public concert had to be called off by the Australian police.

Justin later apologized to his loyal fan-base saying, "I am so sorry that it got out of control. We don't want anyone to get hurt. It gets crazy sometimes."

HEART OF GOLD

To show his fans just how important they are to him, Justin has taken a leaf out of Willy Wonka's book. He has hidden golden tickets in some copies of his CD, *My World 2.0*. The lucky fans who find the tickets will win a trip to the Bahamas with Mr Bieber himself. What a prize!

WORLDWIDE MANIA

In addition to the hordes of screaming fans Justin meets as he travels around the world, he also gets lots of attention on the internet.

Millions have watched his videos on YouTube, and he has over two million followers on Twitter – a popular website where celebrities and fans exchange messages called 'tweets'. He also has more than 880,000 fans on MySpace and over four million followers on Facebook.

JUST LIKE JUSTIN

Go with the flow to find out how you're most like Justin ...

START HERE

Do you have lots of friends – both boys and girls?

YES → Are you a good secret-keeper?

YES → Would you like to be famous one day?

YES → Do you spend ages getting ready to go out?

Are you a good secret-keeper? **NO** → Would you ever eat squid?

Would you like to be famous one day? **NO** → Are you a bit of a flirt?

Are you a bit of a flirt? **YES** → Do you like snowball fights?

Are you a bit of a flirt? **NO** → Do you spend ages getting ready to go out?

Do you like snowball fights? **NO** → Do you spend ages getting ready to go out?

Would you ever eat squid? **NO** → Are you a bit of a flirt?

Would you ever eat squid? **YES** → Are you good at playing video games?

Do you have lots of friends? **NO** → Do you like to stand out from the crowd?

Do you like to stand out from the crowd? **YES** → Would you ever eat squid?

Do you like to stand out from the crowd? **NO** → Have you kept the teddy you had when you were little?

Have you kept the teddy you had when you were little? **NO** → Are you good at playing video games?

Have you kept the teddy you had when you were little? **YES** → Are you a fan of soppy movies?

Are you good at playing video games? **YES** → Do you know lots of songs by heart?

Are you good at playing video games? **NO** → Are you a bit of a flirt?

Are you a fan of soppy movies? **NO** → Do you know lots of songs by heart?

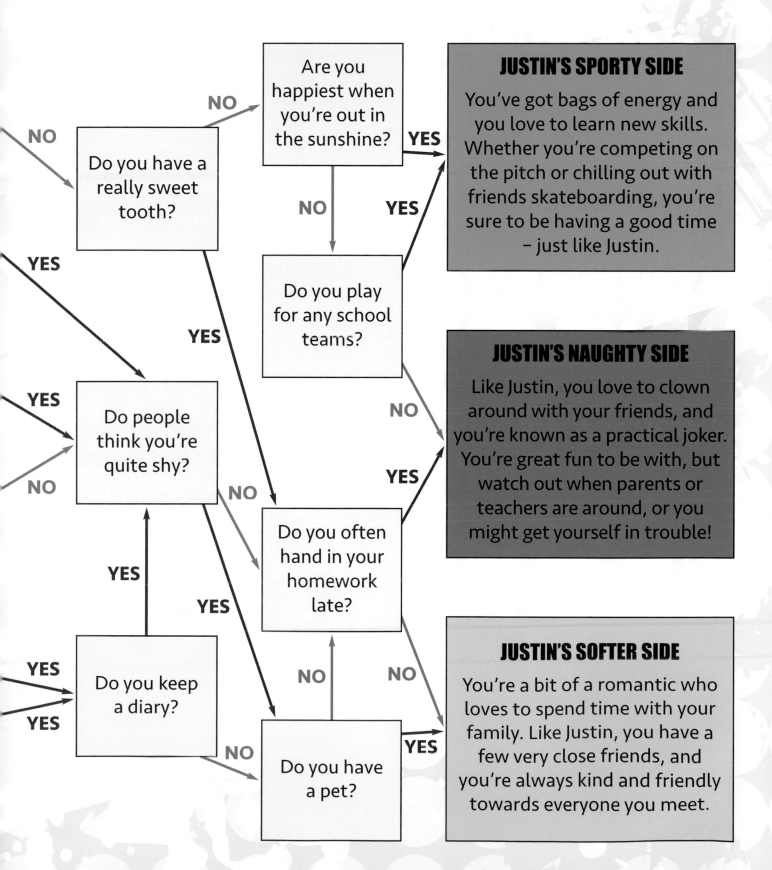

Do you have a really sweet tooth?

Are you happiest when you're out in the sunshine?

Do you play for any school teams?

Do people think you're quite shy?

Do you often hand in your homework late?

Do you keep a diary?

Do you have a pet?

JUSTIN'S SPORTY SIDE
You've got bags of energy and you love to learn new skills. Whether you're competing on the pitch or chilling out with friends skateboarding, you're sure to be having a good time – just like Justin.

JUSTIN'S NAUGHTY SIDE
Like Justin, you love to clown around with your friends, and you're known as a practical joker. You're great fun to be with, but watch out when parents or teachers are around, or you might get yourself in trouble!

JUSTIN'S SOFTER SIDE
You're a bit of a romantic who loves to spend time with your family. Like Justin, you have a few very close friends, and you're always kind and friendly towards everyone you meet.

WRITTEN IN THE STARS

Find out what your horoscope says about you,
and what role you'd be perfect to play in Justin's life.

PISCES

FEBRUARY 20th – MARCH 20th

You're a dreamer with a great imagination. You're shy, but once you feel comfortable you're a real party person.

YOU COULD BE JUSTIN'S: PERFECT MATCH

Justin's a Pisces, just like you. With your creativity and kindness, you really are like two peas in a pod.

GEMINI

MAY 22nd – JUNE 21st

Well, aren't you a charmer? With your silver tongue you can talk your way out of even the stickiest of situations.

YOU COULD BE JUSTIN'S: PUBLICIST

Your confidence and chattiness will help make sure that everyone you meet becomes a Belieber in no time.

ARIES

MARCH 21st – APRIL 20th

You're outgoing and love to be the centre of attention. When you set your mind to something, you usually achieve it.

YOU COULD BE JUSTIN'S: POP RIVAL

If you decide to become a musician, you could well take the charts by storm. Justin had better watch out!

CANCER

JUNE 22nd – JULY 23rd

You like to keep people on their toes, and hate routines. You are very loyal to the people you care about.

YOU COULD BE JUSTIN'S: BODYGUARD

If anyone upsets your fave star they'll be in big trouble. No one will mess with Justin when you're around.

TAURUS

APRIL 21st – MAY 21st

You are trustworthy, and would never reveal anyone's secrets. You're generous and love being with your friends.

YOU COULD BE JUSTIN'S: ADVISER

With your great listening skills and ability to give fantastic advice, you're the one to cheer Justin up whenever he feels blue.

LEO

JULY 24th – AUGUST 23rd

Bubbly and fun, you're happiest when you're creating things and making others laugh.

YOU COULD BE JUSTIN'S: STYLIST

Making sure that Justin always looks his cutest and finding him loads of cool clothes could be the perfect job for you.

VIRGO

AUGUST 24th – SEPTEMBER 23rd

You're a perfectionist who loves to make sure that every detail of any project you tackle is the best it can be.

YOU COULD BE JUSTIN'S: BACKING SINGER

Your support and eye for detail will help make sure that Justin's songs keep on hitting the top of the charts.

SAGITTARIUS

NOVEMBER 23rd – DECEMBER 21st

It's sometimes hard to keep track of you, because you're such a free spirit. You love to be busy and are always on the move.

YOU COULD BE JUSTIN'S: SPORT'S COACH

With your energy and sense of humour, you're sure to keep Justin on his toes both on and off the pitch!

LIBRA

SEPTEMBER 24th – OCTOBER 23rd

Easy-going and great fun to be around, you're a peacemaker who hates to see anyone upset or worried.

YOU COULD BE JUSTIN'S: BFF

You're happy either hanging out at home when Justin's got some downtime, or supporting him at his shows.

CAPRICORN

DECEMBER 22nd – JANUARY 20th

You're reliable, organized and practical. You don't get flustered easily and find that people turn to you in a crisis.

YOU COULD BE JUSTIN'S: ASSISTANT

Your organized approach to life and calm way of facing problems means you could really help Justin out with his schedule.

SCORPIO

OCTOBER 24th – NOVEMBER 22nd

You're intelligent, determined and you don't let things get you down. You're independent and love to be in charge.

YOU COULD BE JUSTIN'S: INTERVIEWER

With your keen mind and probing questions, you'd be the perfect person to get the in-depth scoop on Justin's life.

AQUARIUS

JANUARY 21st – FEBRUARY 19th

Imaginative and patient, you're a creative spirit who tries to get the most out of life.

YOU COULD BE JUSTIN'S: CHOREOGRAPHER

You'd be great at inventing new dance moves for Justin to wow the crowds with. Your inspiring nature will help him to master any tricky steps he tries.

FAMELINE

Justin may be only 16 years old, but he's already had quite a journey in the music industry. Check out some of the most important dates in Justin's life so far.

1st MARCH 1994: Baby Bieber is born in London, Ontario, Canada.

SEPTEMBER 2007: Justin wins second place in the 'Stratford Idol' competition.

OCTOBER 2008: Justin is officially signed to Island Records.

7th JULY 2009: 'One Time', Justin's debut song, hits US radio airwaves.

13th SEPTEMBER 2009: Appearing on MTV's Video Music Awards, Justin performs some of his hit songs and introduces Taylor Swift with Miranda Cosgrove.

17th NOVEMBER 2009: Justin releases *My World*, which includes hits such as 'One Time' and 'One Less Lonely Girl'.

22nd DECEMBER 2009: Justin is awarded a platinum album disc after *My World* sells over one million copies.

18th JANUARY 2010: At the HMV store in London's Westfield Shopping Centre, UK, Justin meets throngs of supporters to sign autographs and greets some of his British fans.

31st JANUARY 2010: Justin presents an award (called a Grammy) at the 52nd Annual Grammy Awards and meets loads of music superstars on the red carpet.

23rd MARCH 2010: *My World 2.0*, Justin's second album, tops the US charts.

27th MARCH 2010: Justin surprises fans at the Nickelodeon Kids' Choice Awards with a musical performance.

28th MARCH 2010: His TV show, *The Diary of Justin Bieber*, premieres on MTV, to give fans a behind-the-scenes look at the pop star's life.

5th APRIL 2010: Justin performs at 'The White House Easter Egg Roll' – an Easter celebration concert. He meets US president, Barack Obama, and the First Lady, Michelle Obama, is seen rocking out to Bieber's tunes.

10th APRIL 2010: In New York, Justin is the musical guest on the hit American TV show *Saturday Night Live* where he meets the comedy star and celebrity host, Tina Fey.

13th APRIL 2010: Justin gets behind the wheel! Just weeks after his 16th birthday, the star gets his driving licence in Atlanta, Georgia, USA.

23rd JUNE 2010: Justin's first headline tour kicks off in Hartford, Connecticut, in the USA.

IN FASHION

When you are in the spotlight, everyone wants to know what you're wearing. Find out how Justin achieves his cool look and 'that' hairstyle.

EASY STYLE

Justin is enjoying experimenting with his look and he admits, "I'm just a kid, so I can rock whatever. In the last year, I think I've developed my style a little as I've built up my swagger." He's shown off some great casual looks that reflect his own style and he won't let anyone tell him how to dress. "This is me," he says. "I wear a hoodie. I'm just easy."

RED-CARPET FLAIR

At MTV's Video Music Awards in 2009, Justin looked cool and confident on the red carpet. Instead of a boring suit or a dull jacket, Justin chose a bright red T-shirt and matching trainers. His favourite dog tags and cross necklace completed his casual look, making Justin the coolest-looking celebrity there.

FASHION FILE

Justin loves to be different and has a keen eye for fashion. He admits, "I'm not a splurger, but I like clothes like G-star, and I really like shoes – I wear Supras a lot. I wear a lot of hoodies, but I also like Alexander McQueen."

GET YOUR SWAG ON

Justin even has a 'swagger coach'. A guy named Ryan Good helps Justin create the style he wants. "It was kind of a joke we had at first. We didn't really know exactly what his role was. I guess he sort of came on as my stylist, to develop what I like. So we kind of made up this swagger coach title and now everyone refers to it. But it's not like he is teaching me how to swagger," Justin explains.

HAIR-RAISING STYLE

So, how does Justin get his amazing relaxed-but-trendy hairstyle in just five minutes? "After I shower, I blow dry my hair and just shake it and it goes like that," he says. And what about his signature hair flip? He says that he flips his sleek fringe out of his face with a head shake because his hair sometimes gets out of place – it must help him see out from under all that hair, too!

STRANGE BUT TRUE?

During Justin's rise to the top, some truly incredible things have happened to him. But don't believe everything you read ... Some of the super-cool stories below are true, but can you spot the fakes? You can check out your Justin knowledge on page 61.

1. Talk-show host Oprah Winfrey compared Justin to Paul McCartney, Frank Sinatra ... and even Elvis!

TRUE OR FALSE?

2. A fan waiting for Justin's arrival at an airport in New Zealand got so excited that she stole his hat.

TRUE OR FALSE?

3. Superstar rapper P. Diddy offered Justin one of his Lamborghini sports cars.

TRUE OR FALSE?

4. Justin's appearance on US TV show, *The Maury Povich Show*, shot Justin into the limelight.

TRUE OR FALSE?

5. Justin was offered a record deal by the cool singer-songwriter Justin Timberlake.

TRUE OR FALSE?

6. Justin is such a hit in the USA that a burger bar has named a cheeseburger after him.

TRUE OR FALSE?

YOUR OWN BACKSTAGE PASS

CONGRATULATIONS!
You've won a golden ticket for a day out with
JUSTIN BIEBER.

Create your own perfect day with your fave singer by completing the story to match your dreams.

Sometimes there will be a selection of words or phrases in brackets to choose from. The rest of the blanks are for you to write in whatever you like. Have fun!

Last night, I, _____ (your name), hung out with Justin Bieber! It was so much fun.

First, we met at _____, and had our photograph taken together. In our photo, Justin was wearing _____ and _____. I _____ (smiled, laughed, made a funny face) for the camera. So did Justin.

After our photoshoot, Justin and I went _____ (skateboarding, to hang out at the beach, to the fairground). He bought me _____ (an ice cream, a cuddly toy, a red rose).

We were hungry after our adventure, so we decided to go to my favourite restaurant for lunch. It's called _____ and they serve lots of yummy stuff. I ordered _____ and Justin had _____.

Next, it was time for Justin to get ready for his big show. He was going to be performing at the _____ (school, park, theatre) in my home town of _____ later that day.

When we arrived, Justin invited me backstage. While he got changed, his crew offered to do my _____ (hair, make-up, nails) and give me a cool outfit to enjoy the show in.

Just as Justin was ready to go out on stage, he panicked. "I can't find my _____," he said. "I can't perform without it!"

Luckily, I knew what to do. I searched everywhere. "Found it!" I said. "It was under the _____ (sofa, guitar case, bin)."

Justin was really happy to have his _____ back.

He got ready and headed out on stage. I got to watch the whole performance from _____ (the front row, backstage, the VIP section). The show was amazing! Justin sang my favourite song: _____:

After the show, I hung out with Justin again. He taught me how to _____ (play his guitar, do a skateboard trick, sing a harmony).

Just when I thought the day was over, Justin's friend _____ rang him. There was going to be a special party at _____. We went to the party and I got to meet my favourite celebrities _____, _____, and _____!

It was the coolest party ever and even better because I went with Justin Bieber!

JUST IN LOVE

Justin is the hottest-looking prince of pop around, and he sings sweetly about love. But what gets Bieber in a fever? Find out all about Justin and romance.

FIRST KISS

Although Justin only admits to having had a couple of girlfriends, he started dating young – aged only 13. "The first date I ever had ... I took the girl out to eat," he remembers. "She was really nice."

And does he remember his first kiss? Yes – it was at a school dance and he thought it was magical.

CELEBRITY CRUSHES

Some celebrity ladies have caught Justin's eye. He has had a crush on American diva Beyoncé since he was just seven years old. "She's hot!" he admits. "She kinda broke my heart when she married Jay-Z."

In a recent interview with MTV News, Justin said that if he could pick any star in the celebrity world to take out on a date, he would choose Meagan Good, and Kim Kardashian, too.

FAN FEVER

Luckily, you don't have to be a star to be Justin's favourite girl. He would happily date a fan, too. "Whoever I fall in love with, you can be anybody. I don't limit myself," he reveals.

READY FOR ROMANCE

Fortunately, Justin has given some tips to the ladies on what he is looking for. He puts a nice smile and pretty eyes at the top of his list. Girls don't need to wear lots of make-up to impress him either. He prefers a down-to-earth girl with a more natural look.

Looks alone are not enough for Justin. His perfect companion must have two qualities – the ability to make him laugh and the intelligence to have a great conversation with him.

FIRST DATE

So what can you look forward to on a date with the delicious Mr Bieber? Well, his ideal night out would be to get something to eat, chat and get to know a girl.

Justin might always get the girl in his videos, but in real life he's shy, "Yeah! If I really like a girl, I get nervous."

The only bad news is that Justin doesn't believe in kissing on the first date, so be patient!

ARE YOU JUSTIN'S NUMBER ONE?

Here's a fast and fun way to work out whether you are Justin's perfect match.

Write your name and his with 'LOVES' in the middle. Then write down how many letter Ls, Os, Vs, Es and Ss there are in both your names in a line. Add together pairs of numbers – the first and the second, the second and the third and so on – to work out a final 'percentage'. This tells you how likely you are to be Justin's number one girl.

Here's an example:
JUSTIN BIEBER LOVES MORGAN LILLY

There are three Ls, one O, zero Vs, two Es and one S.

Write this as:
3 1 0 2 1

Add together each pair of numbers until you have only two left.

4 1 2 3
5 3 5
88%

FAME!

Justin has enjoyed meeting his fans and soaking up life as a celebrity. But how does he handle life in the limelight day to day?

HUMBLE BEGINNINGS

It's hard to imagine, but Justin didn't always think he'd be famous. "I'm from a small town and I never dreamed that posting videos online would change my life," he remembers. "To be in this position at such a young age is just incredible."

FAN-TASTIC!

Justin knows he owes his fame to all his fans and he tries to show them his appreciation by keeping up with them on Twitter and sharing his experiences.

He also makes sure he gives fans the attention they deserve when he meets them. "It's like me meeting Beyoncé," he explains. "I try to give them the best experience that, you know, I would want from someone that I really like."

FANATICAL FANS

Justin has met all kinds of fans, but one of his craziest encounters happened when he walked into a radio station. A girl saw Bieber and ran straight towards him. Instead of giving him a hug, like Justin expected, she tackled him, landing them both on the floor!

Don't worry about Justin too much though – he doesn't mind being surrounded by excited fans. "What 15-year-old wouldn't want screaming girls waiting for him all the time?" he joked in an interview last year.

LIFE-CHANGING FAME

There are definitely some advantages to being famous. "Just being able to travel around the world, I get to see some of the great places and stuff," says the grateful star. "I like being famous because I just get to influence others in a positive way."

FLYING HIGH

Because Justin is so famous, he gets noticed almost everywhere he goes. He reckons the weirdest place that someone has recognized him was high up in the air. Justin recalls, "I was on a plane and these girls were like, 'Are you Justin Bieber?' It was so strange."

CELEB GOSSIP

Scarily, an outrageous, false rumour circulated that Justin had died! This kind of gossip is nothing new – his fellow stars in the music biz, including Taylor Swift and Miley Cyrus, have had similar rumours spread about them online.

The horrible hoax was quickly cleared up, however, when Justin confirmed he was very much alive. "Oh yeah ... and it feels so good to be alive. haha," Justin joked on Twitter.

STARSTRUCK

Even though he is a major celebrity himself, Justin still gets excited when there's a superstar around. Find out which stars he has met and what he really thinks about them.

STARS IN HIS EYES

Justin could barely contain his excitement when he was introduced to two superstars at the music industry's Grammy Awards. He tweeted from the red carpet, "Just met LL Cool J and Smokey Robinson! This is crazy. They knew who I was. Can't believe it."

Justin has met some of the most famous people in the world while touring around, including J.K. Rowling and President Obama, and he even got a kiss on the cheek from singing sensation Rihanna at a party! He joked, "I'll probably never wash my face again."

After being interviewed by talk-show host Oprah Winfrey, an excited Justin exclaimed, "Oprah is real nice down to earth person ... She is incredible ... I can't believe she interviewed me."

SUPER-CRUSH

So how did Justin feel when he got to meet his super-crush, Beyoncé Knowles? "It was amazing. I was a little nervous, but I told her she was very good-looking. Actually she's super hot," says Justin.

Justin has famous friends, too. He describes former tour-mate, Taylor Swift, as an all-round great person.

HOLLYWOOD HYPE

Justin's fans aren't the only ones who have their eye on the hot teen star. Celebs have noticed how talented Justin is, too, and have a lot to say about him.

Can you guess which celebrities said the following things? Pair each of the quotes below to a name in one of the stars, then turn to page 61 to see if you're right!

Rihanna

Tina Fey

1. "Sometimes he's like a little brother or a son to me."

2. "I wish him luck and success. Hopefully his record will do what it's supposed to do."

3. "I like people who can really sing and I think he can really sing."

Taylor Swift

Usher

4. "He broke his foot, on stage in front of 11,000 people, and finished the song!"

5. "He's a cutie pie!"

Kim Kardashian

6. "I officially have Bieber Fever!!"

Snoop Dogg

U SMILE

Justin loves making his fans smile when he's performing, but even when he's off stage, Justin likes to spread the love. One of his dreams is to run his own charity in the future, but for now, he enjoys helping others in any way possible.

HANDS-ON

Justin is a hands-on kind of guy. He designed a necklace for Project Clean Water, a charity foundation established by the singer Jewel. Justin also performed for free at a New York City school to raise money.

"It's very cool. I mean this is what it's all about," says Justin about lending a hand in the community.

FANS IN ACTION

Justin's fans help him achieve his goals when it comes to charities. He asked them to help him raise money for a children's hospital in New York State – and they did. "The fans in Buffalo raised $200k in pennies for charity … that is 20 Million Pennies!!! WOW!! VERY PROUD!!" he tweeted.

GIVING BACK

Justin recently helped to raise money for a selection of charities including Children's Health Fund and Malaria No More. Performing alongside music legends such as Elton John, he lit up the stage on *American Idol's* TV fundraiser show called *Idol Gives Back*.

HELP FOR HAITI

Big stars, including Mary J. Blige and Akon, came out to help fund relief efforts in Haiti, after a terrible earthquake ravaged the country in January, 2010. Justin answered phones at a telethon to raise money and treated fans to a stunning performance on the night. As he wrapped up his hit song, 'Baby', Justin asked for everyone's help, saying, "Donate to Haiti, everybody. Thank you very much. God bless!" He also sang on a charity track called, 'We Are The World', to help raise money for the people of Haiti.

A SPOONFUL OF SUGAR

Justin met some of his fans at a children's hospital in New York, during a visit arranged by the Children's Miracle Network. The star gave personal bedside concerts, and performed his song, 'One Time'. "This is what really matters, and I'm very glad to be here," Justin said. "I just hope they get better soon." Sure enough, his visit to the hospital gave his fans a dose of happiness – just what the doctor ordered.

ON TOUR

Justin has travelled to some amazing places to perform, and he is planning on visiting many more. Here's your all-access pass to find out what life is like on the road with Justin.

AROUND THE WORLD

Justin had one of his first opportunities to sing his heart out when he joined other big stars, such as Kat DeLuna, on the mtvU VMA Tour in 2009.

Later he went to Paris, Japan, New Zealand and Australia to promote his album *My World 2.0*. Justin enjoyed his time abroad and praised his fans on Twitter, saying, "u are all so supportive around the world. thank u."

SHOW SUCCESS

Before he kicked off his first-ever headline tour – the *My World* Tour – in June 2010, Justin was seriously excited. "I think it's gonna be a lot of fun. It's gonna be a big show," he said.

Sure enough, the tour was a sell-out, proving that Justin has a loyal fan-base who love to see him shine on stage. It took him across North America, rocking out at some of the hottest venues in the USA and Canada, including cities such as Los Angeles and Miami.

TOP TOUR MOMENTS

Justin loves being on the road to perform. Here's what he has to say about touring the world:

ON TRAVEL: "The best part [*about being a pop star*] is getting to travel and see the world. I miss my friends, but I love what I get to do."

ON TOURING: "Getting to perform for crowds and fans all around the world. A dream ..."

ON CROSSING THE GLOBE: "Just realized we circled the whole earth with the flights this trip ... Awesome!!" he tweeted this after a whirlwind tour to exciting destinations, including New Zealand and France.

ON DOWNTIME: Justin got to swim with dolphins once while he was touring in the Bahamas in December 2009. "It was one of the coolest things ever," says Justin.

Justin with his mum, Pattie, on the red carpet at the 2010 Grammy Awards.

FAMILY MAN

He may be an international superstar, but Justin keeps his family close to his heart. Read on to find out more about his relationship with his loved ones.

HARDER TIMES

Life hasn't always been easy for Justin and his family. His parents split up when he was very young and he was raised by his mum, Pattie Mallette. "I didn't live in a house that had a lot of money," Justin remembers. "Not having a lot makes me really appreciate what I'm going through right now."

Justin still has a great relationship with his dad, but doesn't get to spend as much time with him as he would like.

BIG BROTHER

Justin is big brother to two younger half-siblings – his sister, Jazmyn, and his baby brother, Jaxon. He loves hanging out with them. He's very protective of his little sister and will stick up for her no matter what. So her future boyfriends had better watch out!

Family is so important to Justin that his biggest 16th-birthday wish was to have them all together and spend time with them ... aww.

THE BEST MUM IN THE WORLD

Justin's mum travels with him, to keep his feet on the ground and make sure that he's happy while on tour. Justin admits that it's not exactly normal for a 16 year old to be around his mum all day, every day. "We bump heads sometimes," he says, "But I have a great relationship with her. She's the best mum in the world."

GIVING BACK

Justin is very grateful to his family for all their support – especially his mum. "She's always there for me," he says, "I never want to let her down."

The successful star knows how tiring travelling can get sometimes, so he treated his mum to a luxury spa break for her birthday. But pampering in a spa is not the only thing big-hearted Bieber has planned to say thank you to his mum for everything she's done for him. As soon as he can, he wants to buy her a house!

PARENTAL PRIDE

Justin's a regular Twitter user, keeping his fans up-to-date with what he's up to, but did you know that both his parents use Twitter, too? They tweet to fellow Beliebers, and let the world know how proud they are of their son.

JUSTIN'S WORLD

Read on to find out what Justin thinks about all the issues in his life, from girls to guitars to, err … golf.

"I'll go out with anyone who I really fall in love with."

"Usher has given me some great advice, stay humble, stay proud and you will go real far with that."

"I think I'm still immature sometimes, but I try not to think I'm hot stuff."

"I'm only 16 once. I've got to live like it."

"Don't believe dreams come true? Think about this – I'm following more people on Twitter than live in my entire hometown. Dreams do come true."

"I used to get nightmares watching Scooby Doo. Not anymore."

"He [President Obama] messed up my name, but I give it to him. He's not the age category I sing to. He's not 'One Less Lonely Girl'."

"When I'm playing my guitar and someone's trying to talk to me I'm just zoned out."

8:18 a.m., 3rd April: "my golf game is unstoppable."

8:27 a.m., 3rd April: "… my golf game has proven to be stoppable … haha."

"'One Time' gets stuck in my head 'cause I have to perform it a lot."

"I'm still the same kid that started on YouTube … still the kid that wakes up everyday feeling blessed to have the fans I have."

"Zac Efron's got nothing on me!"

"Just arrived and I like Australia. I like the weather, the accents, the girls, the water, the excitement, the girls, and the girls."

HALL OF SHAME

Justin's had some amazing – and embarrassing –
moments in the spotlight! Find out some of the things
he'd rather you didn't know about him ...

BREAK A LEG, JUSTIN!

While Justin was on tour with fellow teen singing sensation, Taylor Swift, they were performing at Wembley Arena in London. Taylor wished him luck before the show. "I was like, 'Good luck! It's so good to have you! Break a leg!' ... I wish I'd clarified that," Taylor remembers.

Moments later, as he sang his hit song 'One Time', Justin tripped and fell.

Brave Mr Bieber managed to finish the song he was singing before he was rushed off to hospital. There it was confirmed that Justin had broken his foot. He says it was the most embarrassing moment of his life!

SAUCY DATE?

Justin planned to charm a girl at an Italian restaurant on their first date, but things took a terrible turn when Justin spilled spaghetti all over her! "It was terrible and embarrassing. I never went out with her again. So I would suggest not going out for Italian on a first date because it can be messy! I'll never make that mistake again," Justin says.

TONGUE-TIED

While presenting at the 2010 Grammy Awards, Justin accidentally revealed his crush on the superstar, Beyoncé! He was supposed to remind viewers that they could vote for a Bon Jovi song, but instead Justin muddled his lines, replacing Bon Jovi with Beyoncé. Cringe!

SCHOOL DAYS

Justin was working on a school project, when one of his best friends decided to play a trick on him. As Justin presented his project to the whole class, they started to laugh at him. It turns out that Justin's friend put a really embarrassing picture on top of the project, causing poor Justin to blush. But, there were no hard feelings – the prankster is still one of Justin's best friends.

RACE TO TOP THE CHARTS!

HAVE YOU GOT THE JUSTIN FACTOR?

Do you have what it takes to ride the highs and lows of the music biz like Justin did? Battle your friends for chart-topping sensation status to find out.

HOW TO PLAY

To kick things off, place counters – one for each player – on the 'Start' box. Players must then roll a dice and the person with the highest score starts. Take turns rolling the dice and move your counter the number of spaces shown. You must land on the top box of each section before you can move on to the next stage.

**Your talent has been spotted by a manager in the music business.
Go to STAGE TWO.**

You post your performance on YouTube.
Your videos get millions of hits.
Move forward one space.

Wow! Your singing gets a huge round of applause and you come 2nd.
Move forward two spaces.

A sore throat means you'll have to audition next week. Miss a go.

**You've been signed by one of the biggest record labels in the world.
Go to STAGE THREE.**

A producer wants to sign you to his label.
Roll again.

One of your favourite pop stars flies you over for a meeting.
Move forward one space.

Your family has concerns about you entering the music business.
Move back two spaces.

↑

STAGE ONE:
AUDITIONS FOR SINGING COMPETITION

↑

STAGE TWO:
FIGHT FOR A RECORD DEAL

YOU WIN! Your album has topped the charts all over the world. Congratulations, superstar!

**Your shows are packed with screaming fans who love you.
Go to the FINAL STAGE.**

All the travelling around has left you with some pretty serious jet lag. Miss a turn while you catch some *zzz*.

You do an exclusive photoshoot for a famous magazine and get your picture on the cover. Move forward two spaces.

Your concert tickets sell out.
Roll again.

Whoops! You get an interviewer's name wrong on the radio. Move back three spaces.

You're invited to perform for the President of the USA.
Move forward one space.

Oh no! You break your foot while dancing on stage.
Move back three spaces.

You've got over a million fans following you on Facebook.
Move forward two spaces.

STAGE THREE:
ON TOUR

FINAL STAGE:
WORLD DOMINATION

HOT HOBBIES

He can sing like a superstar, but Justin's talents don't stop there.
What does Justin get up to when he's not on stage?

TALENTED SPORTSMAN

Justin is an up-and-coming star in the basketball stakes. He can spin a ball on his finger like a pro and has even beaten Usher in a game in New York. Justin teased Usher after the game, boasting, "All I know is I'm better than him."

Justin loves golf and was shown on YouTube going wild, screaming, "What a putt!"and punching the air, after tapping a ball into the hole from over six metres away.

TEAM PLAYER

Justin has shown off some serious soccer skills, but his all-time favourite sport has to be ice hockey. He told fans, "I love hockey ... I played hockey all my life."

Justin played ice hockey for a team called the Atlanta Knights and wore sweater number 18. His favourite playing position is centre. His all-time favourite sports player is Wayne Gretzky, former ice-hockey superstar.

SKATEBOARDING STYLE

A dedicated boarder, Justin loves street skating – sliding down handrails and perfecting tricks. He can perform skating tricks, including a '360', an 'Ollie' and a 'kickflip'.

PLAY BALL

At a baseball game in May 2010 with a team called the Chicago White Sox, Justin had the honour of throwing the first pitch (first ball). Later, while he was watching the action, he caught a foul ball that was hit into the spectators' stand by White Sox player, Paul Konerko. Justin tweeted, "Today was epic ... Went to the White Sox game and got to throw out the first pitch ... but the cool part was I caught a foul ball. NO LIE."

SERIOUS SPORTSFAN

Justin's number one team is the Toronto Maple Leafs of the National Hockey League. He tweeted that he is 'leafs for life, true fan'. His favourite basketball team is the Cleveland Cavaliers.

As part of Justin's 16th-birthday celebrations, he was pictured watching a Los Angeles Lakers basketball game, sitting next to Sean Kingston (a recording artist he worked with on *My World 2.0*). At the same time, Justin was following the USA vs Canada Olympic hockey game on TV. He tweeted that day, "Today is a great sports day. Canada for the gold!"

But it seems that the games couldn't hold his attention all the time, as the ladies' man was pictured checking out the cheerleaders in the front row ... naughty Justin!

DANCE MOVES

Aged eight, Justin was filmed busting some killer breakdancing moves at a family party. His dancing has improved with age, and he wowed the crowd with some seriously hot footwork on TV's *CBS Early Show*, filmed on Miami beach.

REGULAR GUY

Justin is just a regular guy at heart and on his days off he loves to lie in bed, watching TV and playing video games.

JUSTIN'S VIDEO DIARY

Since his first appearances on YouTube, Justin has made some really sophisticated videos for his hit singles. Here's some of the behind-the-scenes gossip from the sets.

'ONE TIME'

• Justin's first video and Usher appeared in it. When the cameras weren't rolling, Justin and Usher enjoyed joking around on set.

• Justin's BFF Ryan Butler appears at the start of the video sitting on a sofa playing video games with the star.

'ONE LESS LONELY GIRL'

• Justin didn't have a girlfriend at the time he made this video, and said, "That's why I can kiss this girl."

• In the video, Justin is seen playing with some cute pooches outside a pet store, but then one of them peed on his sneakers!

'BABY'

• Justin explained that this video, shot in a bowling alley, was inspired by Michael Jackson. "We're kind of going off the 'You Make Me Feel' video ... I'm following her around trying to get the girl." Justin also got to show off his moon-walking skills – one of Jackson's signature moves.

• Justin really flirted with actress Jasmine Villegas, his pretty co-star in this video. When she asked him why he was chasing her around the bowling alley, he answered, "Because you are just so gorgeous and you have such a stunning personality."

'NEVER LET YOU GO'

• This video was filmed in an amazing aquarium at the Atlantis resort in the Bahamas.

'EENIE MEENIE'

• Justin worked with Sean Kingston in the video 'Eenie Meenie'. Justin reveals, "The concept of the video is that me and Sean Kingston are getting played by the same girl ... By the end we're like, you know, me and Sean are boys, we don't really want to fight over a girl."

• Justin's other buddie, Christian Beadles, appears in the video, dancing to the music.

HEADING 'UP'

At just 16 years old, Justin has already had an amazing career, but he plans to soar higher and higher. Here are his dreams for the future.

STAY IN THE SPOTLIGHT

Justin is enjoying being in the spotlight, meeting his fans and living out his dreams. In the next five years he hopes to scoop up a prestigious music industry Grammy Award.

HOLLYWOOD CALLS

Justin wants to have a career as an actor. He's already guest-starred in the Nickelodeon film, *School Gyrls*, and his manager is working to get the ambitious teen his own TV show.

GIVE BACK

Justin's not all about living life on stage. The teen sensation also wants to have his own charity by the time he's 17. As he grows, Justin hopes he can inspire others to realize their dreams.

BACK TO SCHOOL

Beyond his life behind the microphone, Justin plans to continue his education. "I want to go to college and just become a better person," he says. "I think I can grow as an artist and my fans will grow with me."

ON TOP

Whatever Justin chooses to do, from being a star student at college to topping music charts all over the world, he knows he couldn't have done it without the support of his family, his friends, his fans and a lot of hard work.

Justin knows what advice he would give other people hoping to head to the top. "Follow your dreams. You can do anything you set your mind to."

With the right attitude and some of the most original talent the music world has seen in a long time, Justin's future is looking very bright.

ARE YOU A BELIEBER?

You love his music, your room is covered in posters of him and you're pretty sure you know everything there is to know about Justin.

So, you're definitely a fan, but are you a true Belieber? Take this quiz and find out. You can check your answers on page 61.

3. What is the name of the Easter concert that Justin performed in at the White House?

a. Sweet Easter

b. Easter Egg Roll

c. Easter Omelette

1. Where is the music video for Justin's smash hit single 'Baby' set?

a. At a theme park

b. In a bowling alley

c. At a zoo

4. Justin has a younger half-brother and half-sister. What are their names?

a. Jason and Jessica

b. Jacob and Jonica

c. Jaxon and Jazmyn

2. What type of dog is Justin's beloved pet, Sammy?

a. A golden retriever

b. A chihuahua

c. A papillon

5. At the MTV Video Music Awards in 2009, which artist was Justin there to introduce?

a. Taylor Swift

b. Justin Timberlake

c. Beyoncé

9. In which Nickelodeon film was Justin a guest star?

a. *School's Out*

b. *School Sucks*

c. *School Gyrls*

6. What are the names of Justin's two best friends from home?

a. Paul and Ryan

b. Christian and Ryan

c. Christian and Jesse

10. Which ice hockey team did Justin play for?

a. The Toronto Maple Leafs

b. The Cleveland Cavaliers

c. The Atlanta Knights

7. During a performance on stage at Wembley Arena in London, what did Justin break?

a. His arm

b. His foot

c. His heart

11. What is hidden inside some of Justin's CDs?

a. A signed photo

b. A lock of his hair

c. A golden ticket

8. In February 2010, a false rumour was spread on the internet. What did it claim?

a. Justin had died

b. Justin was secretly engaged

c. Justin had given up music

12. How many pennies were raised by Justin's fans for a New York State hospital?

a. 20 thousand

b. 20 million

c. 200 thousand

THE LAST TEN

Just when you thought you knew it all, we've got even more fab Justin facts for you.

1. Justin started playing the drums when he was really tiny. His mum let him bang on pots and pans in the house and bought him a drum kit when he was just four years old. Since then, the talented teen has taught himself to play the piano, guitar and trumpet.

2. Justin's super-cute looks, incredible voice and sweet personality are driving girls wild all over the world. If all of these qualities weren't enough, he's also fluent in French, which many people say is the 'language of love' – ooh la la!

3. Before he was famous, Justin would play his guitar on the street to earn some extra cash. He took his mum on a holiday to Disneyland with the money he made.

4. British singer Lily Allen caused a stir when she dissed Justin on Twitter. His devoted fans immediately leapt to his defence.

5. Justin is often seen wearing dog tags and other cool necklaces, but did you know that Justin also has both of his ears pierced? Not a lot of people know this, because he rarely wears earrings.

6. Rihanna was the subject of Justin's cheeky charm. He asked her on a date, but she turned him down for being too young. Aww ... better luck next time.

7. Justin has admitted that the part of his pop star lifestyle that really gets on his nerves is having to get up so early in the morning. Zzzzz.

8. Cool as a cucumber, Justin says he doesn't get nervous when he's performing in front of thousands of people.

9. Justin can be a bit of a daredevil. While on tour in New Zealand, he took part in a bungee jump off Auckland Bridge. Brave Bieber said he wasn't scared at all before making the leap.

10. Justin has impressed many people in the music business with his cool, confident and professional attitude. His mentor Usher said, "Although he's 16, when you talk to him, it's like you're talking to a well-seasoned young man."

ALL THE ANSWERS

STRANGE BUT TRUE? – PAGE 27

1. True! Oprah, queen of the talk show, said that Justin was this generation's 'super heart-throb', just like Paul McCartney, Frank Sinatra and Elvis were for earlier generations – praise indeed!

2. True! Not only did a fan steal Justin's hat from his head, but a crowd also rushed forward to get to Justin and knocked over his mum. Poor Pattie!

3. True! P. Diddy did make this generous offer, but the car never appeared. Justin laughed it off, saying, "He's all talk!"

4. False! Justin was invited to appear on Maury Povich's show, but he turned the offer down. Fans became aware of Justin when his videos were posted on YouTube.

5. True! Justin Timberlake did offer to sign the talented Mr Bieber, but it was Usher's offer that won Justin's heart in the end.

6. False! Justin's a big fan of the US restaurant chain 'In-N-Out Burger', but as yet, the Bieber Burger does not exist.

HOLLYWOOD HYPE – PAGE 35

1. Usher **2.** Snoop Dogg **3.** Tina Fey
4. Taylor Swift **5.** Rihanna
6. Kim Kardashian

ARE YOU A BELIEBER? – PAGES 58 AND 59

Count up your answers and discover whether or not you're a true Belieber in all things Bieber …

1. b **2.** c **3.** b **4.** c **5.** a **6.** b
7. b **8.** a **9.** c **10.** c **11.** c **12.** b

If you scored: 0 – 4

Not there yet! You're on your way to catching Bieber Fever, but you've got some work to do to become a true Belieber.

If you scored: 5 – 7

You know quite a lot about Justin, but there's still room to find out more. Keep up the good work and you'll earn yourself the title of true Belieber soon.

If you scored: 8 – 12

Congratulations! You really know your stuff, and there's no doubt that you're a Belieber. With all those Justin facts in your head, how do you make room for studying?